Fission

Max Gillette

RED MARE
PRESS

This is a work of fiction. Names, characters, places, and incidents are either the product of the author's imagination or are used fictitiously, and any resemblance to actual persons, establishments, events, or locales is entirely coincidental.

FISSION

Copyright © Max Gillette, 2026. A Red Mare Press book.

Published in partnership with *Palette Poetry*, an online literary journal.

All rights reserved.

No part of this publication may be reproduced or reprinted without prior written permission of *Palette Poetry*. To inquire about rights and reprint permissions, please contact *Palette Poetry*.
www.palettepoetry.com / contact@palettepoetry.com

Red Mare Press upholds the right to free expression and recognizes the importance of copyright in fostering creativity. Copyright exists to inspire writers and artists to produce works that contribute to and shape our culture.

Edited by Elyssia Nguyen and Sara Dudo.

Cover design by Emelie Mano.

Interior design by Julianne Johnson.

Red Mare Press / Discover New Art, LLC
70 SW Century Drive, Suite 100442, Bend, Oregon 97702

www.redmarepress.com

Red Mare Press is a division of Discover New Art, LLC.
The Red Mare Press name and logo are trademarks of
Discover New Art, LLC.
The publisher is not responsible for websites (or their content) that are not owned by the publisher.

ISBN 979-8-9939024-2-5

Printed in the United States of America.

CONTENTS

The World is Ending; I Empathize with Vegetables   1

Hydroxyzine Hymn   2

Ode to the Emergency Room   3

Children's Hospital   5

Prayer to the Surgical Technologist   6

Suboxone   7

Nosebleed   8

How Would You Rate Your Pain?   9

Texting my Father from the Pharmacy   11

My Therapist Asks, "Is There Anywhere You Feel Safe?"   12

The World is Ending; I Empathize with Vegetables

To expand the growing season,
farmers trick rhubarb
into flourishing during winter.
The technique is simple: deny
the plant its fiercest need.
Horticulture websites suggest
covering young rhubarb
with a pot, bucket, or similar container
that blocks natural light. Starving,
the rhubarb searches so frantically
for sun that it grows tall enough
to harvest. Frost-stricken mornings,
you can stoop to the ground
and hear the pink stalks stretching.
Blood inside the body
longs to be blood outside the body.
A wound is a window, a hole
for the light to enter.

Hydroxyzine Hymn

I have a piano life—each morning sharper
than the last; every night a sour moon.
Yesterday, a strange doctor spent ten
minutes with me before offering sedatives
and calling for my blood in a slim jar.
I'd like to say I didn't have a pity party,
but lately I've been ashamed of my heart's
slow hardening, its hunched shoulders.
One too many TikToks, collection of quiet
hatred and I fumble for a pill. I want to feel,
but I shrink from pain's shadow like any animal.
I have not learned how to sing terror. Instead,
I listen, and I've learned that dizziness upon standing
isn't so grim when you close your eyes.

Ode to the Emergency Room

Praise the gauze of this place
        wrapped around tubes
        packed into wounds
        slung over beds

Praise the wait on unsteady
benches, the snowmelt halos
of motionless shoes

Praise the emergency contacts
        flushed with panic
        sleepwalking through
        cafeteria and chapel

Praise the ice chips
in Styrofoam cups anointing
the cracked lips
of the dying

Praise the intercom's
        colorful codes

Praise the man
who pushes empty wheelchairs

Praise the CT scanner—*breathe
        in, hold, breathe out, hold*—the MRI
        ultrasound EKG blood draw

Praise the gown, now empty,
stale and crumpled on the bed

Praise the discharge papers
        thumb-worn
        sung-through
        plague psalms

Praise every mess
we leave behind

Children's Hospital

mechanical
arms hover
over every
body. deus
ex machina
(god out
of the machine!)
in the OR.
this stage's
sterile curtains
shift for no
gauze. once
cast, these
bodies can
only loll
and lie
in wait to
be pinned
and picked
apart like
monarch
butterflies
under a
microscope

bluebottle
butterflies
swing from
the lobby
ceiling—glass
shadows cast
waiting parents
in various
shades of
blue. they look
up (a prayer
mirrored in
strings above) to
catch the light
flying from
coiled wings.
their breath
hangs desperate
like glass, like
wire, strung up
two stories
high—fragile
as any child
under a knife

Prayer to the Surgical Technologist

Please, make it quick.
This body's altar
requires no finery.
One sheet—blue
or white—will suffice
for a shroud over
sacrificial steel. Please,
place each instrument
quickly, not far
from cutting hands.
Please, unwrap this body
gently. Let it stay—for a
moment—whole
and warm below
clinical lights. You
guard this place's
stainless chill, but
if you'd like,
you may touch
this body
ungloved.

Suboxone

Ring of decay crowning my left canine,
little canyon above the gum, chalky
and sensitive. The dentist said to expect
more rot and blamed you, my morning
communion, slipped under the tongue.
The residue you leave behind is acidic;
you're corroding my bones. Emerald
ash borer in my bloodstream. Necessary
invader, welcome obliteration. I hate you.
I hate the way my body turns avalanche
without you; muscle and nerve quaking
like pine needles in the bruising cold.

Nosebleed

Just before dawn, she wakes up
choking. A side effect
of the medication. Slick iron
snuffs out all breath in her throat.

She stumbles to the bathroom,
one hand clutching her face.

Down the hall, her parents
rest serene in separate beds.

Pipes in the wall groan dark and low,
the quiet noise of trapped things.

She breathes through her mouth.

Blood drips staccato into the sink
and thickens beneath her fingernails.

Her head hangs over the basin,
neck outstretched, anticipating the ax.
Like a lover, blood finds the flesh
most desperate for attention.

How Would You Rate Your Pain?

0. No Hurt:

2. Hurts a Little Bit:
Gnat-like nuisance of flesh. Cicada fluttering under the skin.
Summer's purple thrumming before a storm—gentle June warning
in the form of heat lightning. Condensation on a glass pitcher. The
first slipped stitch. Deep breath before the squall.

4. Hurts a Little More:
    Warning: volume may   hearing damage. Cover   ears
and pray.   Hard to say   what anyone's saying
    these days   Nerve impulses fire   a fraction of a
volt. Don't   fight the current   better men than you
    drowned.

6. Hurts Even More:
firing   chemical flow   all of us,   more animal
    human   problem
  synapses   wrong   fast   more animal   howl

8. Hurts a Whole Lot:

stranger   tethered   pulse

              jaw   keen

pinch
              shroud   bite   dusk

10. Hurts the Worst:

Texting my Father from the Pharmacy

I'll be better by Thanksgiving

I know you detest those
who seek refuge in prescription

but I lack the patience for meditation,
journaling, or hour-long bubble baths

I am insatiable—I inherited that from you

Today I nearly lunged across the counter
to lick Lexapro dust from the pharmacist's fingertips

Panicked apathy

I cannot accept the desolation
which is my birthright

Every month I'll uncurl my fists
to beg for chemical comfort

The next time you see me
I'll have swallowed so much joy
I could be your sun

My Therapist Asks, "Is There Anywhere You Feel Safe?"

And I think of Chernobyl April 26, 1986.
There is serenity in fucking up that bad.
I imagine Leonid Toptunov, 26
and recently promoted, working the night shift.
Running the safety tests.
Noticing a dangerous drop in power.
Pressing the big orange button and
patting himself on the back
for shutting the reactor off
just in time.

In the months after the accident, hundreds
of thousands were called upon to clean
the site. Those with no military training
were sent to kill all domesticated animals
in evacuated settlements. Dogs and cats
were burned or buried in mass graves
because they posed a threat
to the humans that collared and fed them.

Radiation changes you, mangles
your DNA. Overdose, and your blood vessels
split open like warm spring. There is no cure,
only waiting for each cell to forget
its purpose. A slow un-making, moment
by moment, until you are scalded
from the inside.

When my therapist says "peace is unbearable
to the individual who only knows pain,"
I think about nuclear fission, about how
sometimes, the best I can do is shatter.

ACKNOWLEDGMENTS

Arkana: "Kitchen"

Sage Cigarettes Magazine: "Texting my Father from the Pharmacy"

JAKE, The Anti-Literary Magazine: "How Would You Rate Your Pain?"

Moss Puppy Magazine: "Prayer to the Surgical Technologist"

www.ingramcontent.com/pod-product-compliance
Lightning Source LLC
Chambersburg PA
CBHW071259140726
47996CB00007B/2906